The Amstra

Peter Gosling

Pitman

Computer Handbooks

The complete list of titles in this series and the Pitman Pocket Guide series is available from Pitman Publishing. The Publishers would welcome suggestions for further additions and improvements to the series. Please write to Peter Brown at the address given below.

PITMAN PUBLISHING
128 Long Acre, London WC2E 9AN

© Writers Unlimited 1987
First edition 1987

British Library Cataloguing in Publication Data

Gosling, P. E.
 The Amstrad PC1512.—(Microcomputer handbooks).
 1. Amstrad PC1512 (Computer)
 I. Title   II. Series
 004.165   QA76.8.A4

ISBN 0 273 02819 7

Printed in Great Britain at the Bath Press, Avon

Contents

Acknowledgements

The author wishes to thank Anglia Telecommunications Ltd of Market Deeping, Midland Micro Services of Stamford, Locomotive Software Ltd and Michael Joyce Consultants for their help in the preparation of this Handbook.

Photographs by Patrick Gosling.

How to Use this Handbook

Since this Handbook series was commenced the market for Personal Computers (PCs) has grown dramatically largely due to the influence on the market exerted by the introduction of the IBM PC. This has resulted in the design and manufacture of many machines compatible with the IBM PC and the latest of these 'clones' is the Amstrad PC1512. Its low price, the wide range of software available, and its ease of use have made it a very attractive proposition for installation in small business environments where previously the use of a computer would have been unthinkable.

This Handbook gives a concise account of the facilities offered by the PC1512, both in its hardware and software. It aims to present the information needed by the new user, who probably has never laid hands on a computer keyboard before, in a concise and readable form. Computer manuals are all very well if you are used to using them or have a very clear idea of what you are looking for. The information contained in this Handbook provides you with a compact reference guide to your Amstrad PC. There is some technical information, but not so much as to make it a technical manual. There is just sufficient to give you essential information that you can expand on, should you wish, by reference to the manufacturer's manuals.

The main sections of this Handbook cover the facilities offered on the four Master disks supplied with the machine. Each command in the two Disk Operating Systems (DOS) is explained. The use of

GEM (Graphics Environment Manager) is explained in its context so that you can use your Amstrad PC in an economical manner.

You are supplied with a version of the BASIC (Beginners All purpose Symbolic Instruction Code) interpreter by Locomotive – known as BASIC2 – so that you can, if you wish, write your own programs. The commands in BASIC and their use are listed together with examples of their use.

Among the software available specifically for the Amstrad PC is WordStar 1512 which is a version of the very popular wordprocessing program from MicroPro designed to make use of the facilities offered by your Amstrad PC. The main features of this program are described in this Handbook.

Introducing the Amstrad PC1512

The Amstrad PC1512 series of IBM compatible personal computers all use the Intel 8086 processor chip running at 8MHz and are supplied with 512Kbytes of RAM and a mouse. The models available can have one or two 360Kbyte floppy disk drives or one 360Kbyte drive and either a 10Mbyte or 20Mbyte integral hard disk drive. The floppy disk drives are 40 track, double sided with nine sectors per track. All systems can be delivered with either a monochrome or colour monitor screen. Three expansion slots to take IBM type expansion cards are available. A standard IBM-style keyboard is provided. In the top of the system box, which contains the disk drives, is a compartment to hold the four dry cells that are used to power the non-volatile RAM. This is a 'phantom' disk drive that utilises part of the memory (RAM) as a very fast storage device. Normally with such things the data stored is lost when the power is switched off. This is not the case with the PC1512. The dry cells ensure that data stored in this 'drive' is preserved until the next time you switch the system on.

All existing PC software should run on this machine as well as certain pieces of software written exclusively for it, such as the GEM package and WordStar 1512.

One of the more interesting features, to the new user at least, offered by this machine is the 'mouse'. This is a device consisting of a ball fixed under a small pad which, when used in conjunction with the GEM system, can allow you to select options from the GEM screen by moving the mouse over your desktop, rolling it along, until the moving arrow on the screen is over the representation of the operation you wish to perform. The selection is confirmed by pressing a button on the top of the mouse, thus saving typing time and reducing the errors resulting from the fumbling fingers of the novice user.

THE FOUR MASTER DISKS

1 MS-DOS Version 3.2

Your Amstrad PC1512 uses two operating systems one of which is MS-DOS (Microsoft Disk Operating System) Version 3.2. The other is Digital Research's DOSPlus. Both operating systems will run the common applications programs. The addition of a hard disk to your system enables you to store more program and data files, which can be used by either operating system.

MS-DOS is the operating system located on the first of the four master disks supplied with your machine. In order to get your PC1512 up and running you will need to place this disk in the left hand floppy disk drive of a twin disk machine and switch it on. If you have a single disk drive then you have no option about the drive from which you start. This operation is called, by the way, 'booting up the system'.

If you have a hard disk PC1512 you must first of all format the hard disk and install both operating systems onto it. Your manual will tell you how to do this. Once your hard disk has been installed and formatted soon after switching on your PC you are given the choice of the operating system you wish to use. Press the F1 key for MS-DOS or the F2 key for DOSPlus. Switching on the PC automatically starts the 'booting up' if you have a hard disk installed.

An operating system is a program that enables you to 'talk' to your computer and it to 'talk' to you. The prompt that tells you that it is awaiting your instructions will be a a letter, A, B or C followed by this sign, >, that

5

tells you the name of the disk drive you are logged on to. The drives are referred to as A and B for the two floppy disk drives and C is the non-volatile RAM disk. When you have a hard disk drive installed this is designated drive C and the single disk drive is known (rather confusingly) as both A and B. The RAM disk is set up automatically by the operating system when you start up your PC1512. A prompt will look like

    A>

or

    B>

or

    C>

To change the logged disk drive simply type the name of the drive you wish to use followed by a colon. So that

    A>B:
    B>

will be the sequence if you are orginally logged onto drive A and you wish to be logged onto drive B.

If you need to 'reboot' your PC without switching it off and then switching on again (a practice not to be recommended) then you can perform a 'warm boot' by pressing the Control, Alt and Del keys simultaneously.

Built-in Commands

MS-DOS contains a number of command words that you can type in so that you can make the operating system perform a number of tasks for you. The first set are what are termed *built-in commands* with the operating system. These are:

BREAK can be set ON or OFF in order to disable the Control-C function. Control-C (the Control key and C pressed simultaneously) is the usual way to interrupt the execution of any MS-DOS command. Should you wish to disable Control-C then you use the command

    BREAK OFF

To enable Control-C the command is

    BREAK ON

BREAK on its own will display the current setting of the command.

CHDIR or CD will allow you to change directories. For example:

    CD \WP

will move you from the root (main) directory into a directory called WP – possibly for wordprocessing.

CD \ will move you from a sub-directory back into the root directory.

CLS will clear the screen for you.

COPY is the command used to allow you to make a copy of one or more files. For example:

    COPY SALES?.CAL B:

will copy all the files with five character names beginning with SALES and with .CAL extensions from the current directory onto the disk in drive B:. The COPY command is always in the form of

    COPY <sourcefilename> <targetfilename>

and the current logged disk drive is always assumed to the required drive if a drive is not otherwise specified.

CTTY allows you to alter the device on which you are working so that you can direct the input or output to one of the following devices:

AUX   – a device connected to the serial (RS-232C)port.
CON   – the console (input via keyboard; output via screen).
PRN   – a printer connected to the parallel printer port.
NUL   – a non-functional device. Used during development of a program.
LPT1   – same as printer.
COM1 – communications port – same as AUX.

The form of the command is, for example:

    CTTY PRN

DATE allows you to set the date in the form DD.MM.YY

DEL or ERASE will delete one or more files from a specified disk.

Note: Use of wildcard characters. The characters ? and ✶ can be included in file names where the ? stands for any single character and ✶ for any number of characters.

✶.COM stands for any file with a .COM extension

SALES? stands for any file with a name such as SALES1, SALES2, etc, but not SALES10.

DIR will provide you with a directory listing of all the files stored on a specified disk. A file name can be prefixed by a drive name followed by a colon followed by the name that can consist of up to eight characters, spaces not allowed, and an 'extension'.

DIR/W will list a directory across the screen rather than in a vertical list.

DIR/P will display one screenful of file names and will halt to allow you to read them. Press any key to display another screenful.

ECHO is a batch processing command. ECHO OFF prevents batch commands from being echoed on the screen. ECHO ON will switch this feature on again. You can ECHO a message so that

ECHO – Now you are going into the Word Processor

will display that message on the screen when it comes to that line in a batch file.

FOR is used when in a batch file. It allows you to repeat a series of batch operations. An example of this would be

    FOR %%F IN (WP1 WP2) DO MKDIR %%F

which creates two new subdirectories called WP1 and WP2. What happens is that the variable called %% followed by any non-numeric character is put in turn equal to each member of the set whose names are enclosed in brackets. Then the MS-DOS command is used on the resulting argument.

    FOR %%C IN (*.BAT) DO DIR %%C

will list every batch file in the current directory on the disk.

If this command is used outside a batch file then only one % sign is needed.

GOTO is another batch file command that controls looping. It enables control to be passed to the part of the file that starts with a named label. For example:

    :MARK
    ECHO Here we are again
    GOTO MARK

will produce an infinite loop that can only be escaped from by pressing CONTROL and C.

IF is used in a batch file to make a conditional branch if some condition is fulfilled.

MKDIR or MD followed by a name will create a new sub-directory.

PATH is used to indicate which directories are to be examined to find external commands if they do not exist in the current directory.

    PATH\TEST\SUB1;\TEST1\SUB2

will cause the current directory to be searched followed by TEST\SUB1 and then TEST\SUB2.

PAUSE will halt the execution of a batch file until a key has been pressed.

PROMPT allows you to alter the usual MS-DOS prompt. For example if you type the command

    PROMPT Enter a command pg

the usual prompt of

    A>

will be replaced with

    Enter a command A:\>

displaying the text followed by the current directory and the > sign.

RENAME or REN will allow you to rename a file by using the command

    REN <oldfilename> <newfilename>

Groups of files can be renamed by using the ? or * wildcard characters.

REM prefixes a remark in a batch file. If ECHO has been set ON the remarks are displayed on the screen. With ECHO OFF they are not displayed.

RMDIR will remove a directory from a disk, but only if it is empty of all files.

SET is used within MS-DOS batch files to set parameters to specific values. For example, if your batch file contained the line

    DIR %FILE%.DOC

then the command

    SET FILE=SALES?

will set the filename to be the specified set of names and all files of the specified form will be listed. In addition you can assign a new prompt permanently by the command

    SET PROMPT=pg

The SET command on its own will list all commands that have been SET.

SHIFT is used to shift batch file parameters one place to the left.

TIME sets the current time of day in the form hh:mm:ss.

TYPE displays the contents of a file on the screen. It should only be used if the file is in ASCII format. Trying to TYPE a system file or a program file will result in strange displays on the screen and will quite possibly crash your computer system. If you press Control-P after issuing the TYPE command and before pressing the Return (Enter) key you will send the output to the printer as well as the screen. A further Control-P command will switch your printer off.

VER displays the version number of the operating system; 3.2 in the case of the Amstrad PC1512.

VERIFY can be set ON or OFF in order to verify that a file is written correctly to disk.

VOL displays the volume label of the disk in a specified drive. The volume label can be assigned when the disk is formatted and cannot be changed except by reformatting the disk.

    VOL A:

will display the label, if there is one, of the disk in drive A.

External commands

The other MS-DOS commands that exist as separate programs are known as *external commands*:

ANSI.SYS is the screen driver that loads the default screen attributes from the RAM disk where they are kept. It is loaded from the program ANSI.COM in order to reload these attributes in a case where the screen driver has been corrupted.

APPEND sets up a search path for data files, such as

    APPEND B:\file1;B:\file2

ASSIGN assigns a drive letter to another drive. The command

    ASSIGN B=C

means that all references to drive B: are directed to drive C:. There then can be no direct references to drive C:.

ATTRIB sets file Read-Only and Archive attributes. The switches are /+R for Read-Only, /−R for Read-Write, /+A forces backup and /−A stops automatic backup. A typical command would be

    ATTRIB /+R/+A filename

ATTRIB ∗.∗ will display the current file attributes.

CHKDSK allows you to discover the status of a disk and produce a report of the number of files it has stored. In addition it will allow you to discover if there are any errors in the directory and the files and can fix these if required. The /F (Fix) switch at the end of the command will allow CHKDSK to fix any errors it finds. The /V (Verify) switch will display the name of each file on the disk as it comes to it.

COMP will compare two files; line by line for text files and byte by byte for binary files.

DEBUG is used in conjunction with programs that you have written yourself. It enables you to check them for errors ('debug' your programs).

DISKCOMP is used to compare sectors of one disk with those on another. If you perform a sector-by-sector comparison you can tell if one disk is an exact copy of another. It should only be used to compare one floppy disk with another.

DISKCOPY is the command used when you need to copy the entire contents of one floppy disk onto another. If the target disk is blank but not formatted DISKCOPY will format it for you. The copying can be made from one drive to the other on a twin floppy drive PC or from one disk to another on a single drive machine. The usual form of the command will be

    DISKCOPY A: B:

in order to copy the contents of the disk in drive A onto the disk in drive B. If you leave out the drive names the copying is performed on the logged drive only.

EDLIN is the MS-DOS line editor. It is the very simplest kind of text editor you can have, working as it does on a line-by-line basis. It is, however, quite complicated to use and a full description of its use is found in the manual supplied with your PC. Generally speaking it is probably easier to do any editing using a full text editor such as WordStar or the special version developed for your Amstrad – WordStar 1512.

EXE2BIN is a program that converts an external, that is a file with a .EXE extension, into a binary file.

FDISK is the program to configure your hard disk.

FIND is the command to locate all the lines in a specified file that contain a certain string of characters. It will cause each line to be displayed as it is found.

FORMAT is used to format a blank floppy disk, or reformat a previously used disk. The usual form of the command will be

FORMAT B:

if you wish to format the disk in drive B. There are several switches available after the command.

/B reserves a system area on the disk so that an operating system can be written onto the disk at a later date using the SYS command.

/V provides a prompt to ask for the volume label.

/S copies the operating system onto the disk in order to create a 'bootable' disk.

GRAFTABL loads a special table of graphics characters while in graphics mode. This table remains in memory until your PC is switched off or reset.

GRAPHICS enables exact screen images to be copied onto your printer.

JOIN joins a disk drive to a disk directory so that

JOIN C: B:\path

will join C: with the directory structure of A:. In order to break the join the command is

JOIN C:/D

KEYBUK is the command to tailor your keyboard to United Kingdom standards. Other keyboard commands are

    KEYBFR (France)
    KEYBGR (Germany)
    KEYBIT (Italy)
    KEYBSP (Spain)

LABEL creates or amends a disk label by the command

    LABEL drive:label

MODE will change the settings of the various input and output ports.

MORE is what MS-DOS calls a *filtering* command and allows you to display what might well be a lengthy display one screenful at a time. If you do not include a MORE command you will find that the important information you are looking for has flashed by before you have had a chance to read it. An example of this would be

    DIR *.DOC ¦ MORE

so that when you have a complete screenful displayed the prompt

    --MORE--

appears at the bottom of the screen and you will have to press the Return (Enter) key before the next screenful is displayed.

PRINT will allow you to print a set of documents in the background while allowing you to continue with other work in the foreground. A typical print queue is set up as follows

   PRINT SALES1.DOC GRAPH1.PRN SALES2.DOC/P

The /P switch is the signal to start printing. Two other switches are

/T to terminate the print queue

/C to cancel the printing of the specified file.

RECOVER gives you the chance to check and recover any corrupted files. A particular file can be recovered by typing the command followed by the filename. A disk can be recovered if you type RECOVER followed by the drive identifier.

REPLACE will substitute the latest version of a file for an earlier version on your back-up disk.

RTC will enable your settings of time and date to match the system clock; especially for applications programs that make use of the system date and clock.

SHARE installs file sharing and locking; used particularly in multi-user systems.

SORT is another filtering command. It can be used to sort any set of data but is very useful in providing a sorted list of the contents of a directory. By using the command in conjunction with MORE we can produce the listing one screenful at a time by

DIR *.* ¦SORT¦MORE

SUBST will rename a path as a disk drive.

SYS will transfer the hidden files forming part of the MS-DOS program. It will normally be used to transfer such files onto an already formatted disk (one that has been created with the /B switch on when the disk was formatted) or to place an updated version of DOS onto a disk. The command must be followed by the drive identifier of the disk onto which the system is to be copied.

TREE will display a complete list of the directories on the specified disk. If it is used with the switch /F then the files within each directory are listed as well.

XCOPY copies a source file and the structure of the directory onto another disk.

Editing command lines

You can edit any command line, that is any string of commands entered from a DOS prompt, by use of the function keys F1 to F5.

Any command you enter is always stored in memory and can be recalled one character at a time by pressing the F1 key. This enables you to enter the same command again without having to retype it. The same result can be obtained by pressing the → key.

Press F2 followed by a character in the command line and the stored command up to that character becomes the new command.

Press F3 to copy the rest of the stored command onto the command line.

Press F4 followed by a character to skip the copying of the stored command up to that character.

F5 will create a new command line in memory. You would use this if you had realised that you had made a typing error in a long command line before you had pressed Return (Enter). Press F5 instead and then you can correct the line by overtyping, pressing F1 to enter one correct character at a time from the stored command line and then pressing F3 to copy the rest of the original command line into the new one. Pressing F5 will display an @ sign so that if the display looked like this

    A>FORNAT B:/S

you could press F5 before pressing Return so that you get

    A>FORNAT B:/S@

and then by using the F1 and F3 keys you would have this

    A>FORNAT B:/S@
       FORMAT B:/S

You can then press Return and the command will be executed.

The Del, Ins and ← keys can also be used to help with the editing of command lines.

Note: If you want to create your own batch files you can do so by using the COPY command in a special way. All you have to do is to type

    COPY CON: batchfilename.BAT

and type the commands, one per line, terminating with the special control character obtained by pressing CONTROL and Z together. This ensures that the commands coming from the console (your keyboard) are copied into the batch file you have specified.

For example, if you have a subdirectory called WP where the WordStar wordprocessing program is kept you can create a batch program to take you there, and back again into the root directory when you have finished, by means of a batch program called WP.BAT. It would look like this

```
ECHO OFF
CD \WP
WS
CD \
ECHO ON
```

so that all you need to do is to type WP when you are in the root directory and the batch file will do the rest for you. Notice how the batch program contains the DOS commands you would have to have typed in order to produce the same result.

2 GEM Startup

GEM (Graphics Environment Manager) is a system that runs under the Digital Research DOSPlus operating system.

Before using GEM it has to be loaded from the second of the four master disks. GEM is the system which makes the greatest use of the 'mouse' supplied with your PC1512. All you have to do is to place the disk in drive A and close the drive door. If your machine is already switched on press the three keys marked **Control**, **Alt** and **Del** in order to start the operation of reading the program from the disk ('booting' the system up). After a few seconds you will see the message

Loading DOSPLUS.SYS....

After a time the screen will display as shown in Figure 1. If you want to continue move the arrow, by moving the mouse over your desk top, until it is over the **OK** sign. Remove the Startup disk and replace it with the third disk, called the Gem Desktop disk. Press the left hand button of the mouse to set things in motion and watch the screen.

Figure 1

3   GEM Desktop and BASIC2

The GEM Desktop environment presents you with a series of *icons* spread over the screen. These are identified by you when you move the arrow by moving the mouse. Selections are made by what GEM calls 'clicking'. This is a command sent to GEM via the buttons on the mouse. There are four ways in which you can perform the 'clicking'. The first is a single click of the left hand button. This selects an icon on the screen. In other words you move the arrow to the selected icon and click once. If an icon has been selected this way then it can then be opened via the FILE menu.

The second command is the 'double click' which opens an icon, i.e. a document represented by an icon, for use. Two clicks in quick succession are what is required for this. The 'double click' rate can be changed by you if required. This is an alternative to selecting an icon with a single click, which results in the icon being highlighted, and then opening the file from the FILE menu.

The third use of the mouse is to mark a line around a set of icons by pressing the left hand button down and moving the mouse so that a straight line is drawn. This can be used to 'collect' together a series of icons for a collective move for example.

Fourthly, an icon can be deleted by what GEM calls 'shift clicking', holding down the right hand button and pressing the left hand button. This is the same as pressing the Shift key down and clicking the left hand button.

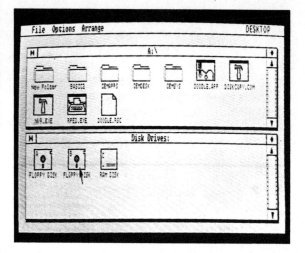

Figure 2

The icons on the screen, as shown in Figure 2, are of several types. There are the floppy disk symbol, the hard disk or RAM disk symbol, a 'folder' which is GEM's name for a subdirectory, a program to be run from the desktop and a data document. The shape of the icon is very clearly indicative of its type.

The windows used by GEM have certain special symbols in their borders. In the top left hand corner is the 'bow-tie' shaped sign which when selected and clicked will close the window. In the top right hand corner is the Full Box sign, a diamond, which when selected will cause the window to fill the screen completely. Figure 3 shows one of the boxes expanded to take up all the screen.

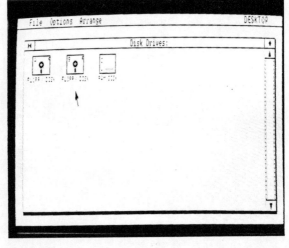

Figure 3

If you want to copy the contents of a folder, say from drive A to drive B, then move the pointer to the folder to be copied, click the left hand button and keep it down. On moving the mouse the arrow becomes a hand and you move this until it covers the icon representing the target drive. On the button being released the special screen is displayed telling you the number of files to be copied and asking for instructions to go ahead. It looks like this:

```
COPY FOLDERS / ITEMS

Folders to Copy:    1
   Items to Copy:   5


             OK     Cancel
```

The copying then takes place automatically when you have selected **OK**.

Across the top of the window is the Title Bar telling you what directory and disk you are looking at. Across part of the bottom and the right hand border of the window are the Scroll Bars. These tell you what part of the window and what proportion of it are being viewed at the time.

You will see along the top of the screen a list of four menu choices.

They are

File Options Arrange   DESKTOP

In order to select one of these move the pointer by moving the mouse and when the arrow points to the choice you have made, click the mouse once.

Desktop

When this is chosen the *Desktop Accessories* are displayed. An option from this menu is chosen by moving the arrow to the required selection and clicking the mouse again.

```
Desktop Info...

Calculator
Clock
Print Spooler
```

Calculator provides you with a picture of a pocket calculator that can be used in the normal way. Move the arrow to the button required and click the mouse. The calculator is shown in Figure 4.

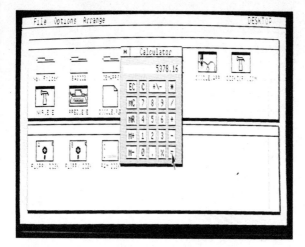

Figure 4

Clock is used like any other digital clock and has an alarm feature built in.

Print Spooler allows printing to take place in the background while you are using another GEM program in the foreground.

Snapshot is another alternative given in the manual, but not on the screen of the system used to produce this Handbook. This is intended to provide an instant 'picture' of a screen or part of a screen that can be printed at your request.

File

```
File

Open
Info/Rename
*************
Delete
Format
*************
To Output
Exit to DOS
```

Open can only be used when a folder, an application or a disk icon, has been highlighted.

Format – NOT AVAILABLE

To Output allows you to print copies of files created by GEM Write and GEM Paint.

Exit to DOS allows you to leave the GEM environment and return to the DOSPlus operating system.

Options

The Options menu relates to a series of DOS disk commands:

```
Options

Install Disk Drive
Configure Application
*********************
Set preferences
Save Desktop
Enter DOS Commands
```

Install Disk Drive allows you to install a new disk drive, or remove one if required, in the system. It is this that would be used if you decided to upgrade your PC1512 by the addition of a hard disk.

Configure Application allows you to install a new application into the GEM system. You can associate a style of icon with the application and all files associated with it.

Set Preferences makes it possible for you to set, for example, the acceptable speed with which double clicks on the mouse can be made.

Save Desktop allows you to make the GEM Desktop fit your requirements and save any changes you may have made to the desktop while you have currently been working with GEM.

Enter DOS Commands is a temporary way out of GEM so that you can perform some specialised work in the operating system. This is sometimes called *shelling out* and you can return to where you were in GEM by typing **Exit** at the DOS prompt.

Arrange

This has the following menu:

```
┌─────────────────────────┐
│  Arrange                │
├─────────────────────────┤
│  Show as Icons          │
│  Show as Text           │
│  *************          │
│  Sort by Name           │
│  Sort by Type           │
│  Sort by Size           │
│  Sort by Date           │
└─────────────────────────┘
```

Show as Icons will have a single tick beside it by default. It denotes that the contents of the current disk or folder are represented by icons.

Show as Text can be chosen if you wish to have no icons displayed but only the more conventional list of files as shown in Figure 5. A tick is shown beside this if it has been selected.

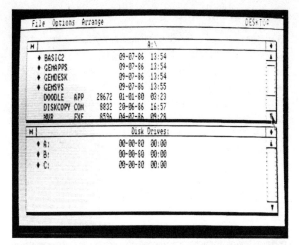

Figure 5

Sort by Name sorts the contents of the window alphabetically.

Sort by Type sorts the files in the window in alphabetical order of their extensions. This means that all the .APP files will come before the .EXE files and before the .TXT files.

Sort by Size sorts the contents of the window according to the number of bytes taken up by each file.

Sort by Date sorts the contents of the window into date order.

33

Locomotive BASIC2

In order to use the BASIC interpreter you will first of all have to load the GEM Startup disk, type the GEM command and then replace this disk with the GEM Desktop disk. When the GEM desktop icons appear move the mouse until the arrow points to the BASIC2 folder and then double click the left hand mouse button. The screen changes and a large **B** named **BASIC2.APP** appears in the middle of the top half of the screen, as shown in Figure 6. Double click the left hand key on the mouse again. You have now selected BASIC2. Across the top of the new screen are seven options

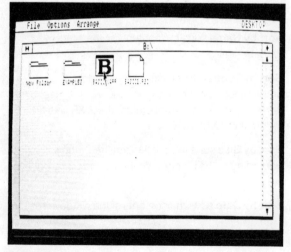

Figure 6

with **BASIC2** in the top right hand corner. The screen
will now be divided into three windows as shown in
Figure 7. In fact, there are four windows available to
you. They are windows onto what are called *virtual
screens*. The **DIALOGUE** window displays the
commands you use to control BASIC, the **EDIT**
window is where you enter your BASIC program
instructions and the **RESULTS-1** (and **RESULTS-2**)
windows can be used for output.

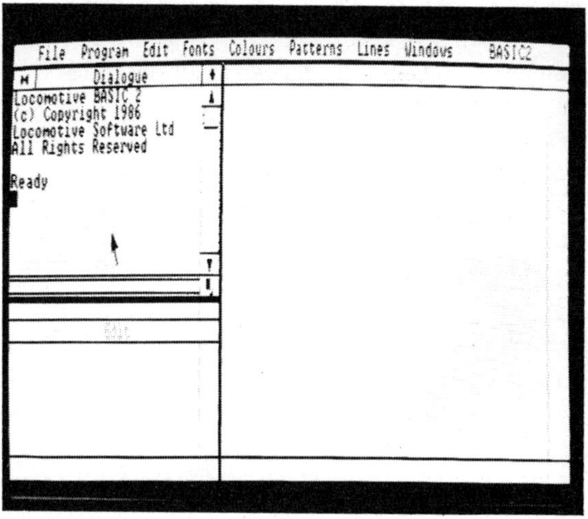

Figure 7

35

On the border of each window there are the 'Close Window' symbol at the top left and the 'Full Box' symbol at the top right. There is also an arrow at the top right, and one at the bottom right of the window which when selected allow you to move the window around the screen. The small rectangular sign at the bottom right hand corner of the screen allows you to change the size of the window by 'dragging' the border around the screen. The up and down arrows at the right of a window allow you to scroll through it and display any contents of the window that are hidden from your view. Place the mouse so that its arrow sits on one of these two symbols and click. The window will scroll. This is because the window may not be large enough to display everything at one time. The menus offer a series of options as detailed below. Any options displayed on the screen in light type are not yet available. The menus are:

```
┌─────────────────────┐
│ File                │
├─────────────────────┤
│ Load . . .          │
│ Save . . .          │
│ * * * * * * * * * * *│
│ Quit                │
└─────────────────────┘
```

```
Program

Run            F9
Stop           Ctrl-C
Continue       F7
*********************
Edit           F10
List                          Lists to the printer
*********************
New
*********************
Angles in ...                 Sets degrees or
                                        radians
```

```
Edit

Exit Edit      F10
****************
Start area     F1
End area       F1
Cancel area    F2
****************
Copy area      F3
Move area      F4
Delete area    F5
****************
Insert off     Ins           * See top of p. 38
****************
Renumber ...                  Only numbered lines
```

* Select and click, or press the **Ins** key to allow you to edit BASIC2 programs by inserting extra lines into the program.

```
┌────────────────────────────┐
│ Fonts                      │
├────────────────────────────┤
│                            │
│   1 System                 │
│   2 Swiss                  │
│   3 Dutch                  │
│   9 Loadable               │
│ ******************         │
│   7 Point    18 Point      │
│   8 Point    20 Point      │
│  10 Point    24 Point      │
│  12 Point    28 Point      │
│  14 Point    36 Point      │
│  16 Point    72 Point      │
│ ******************         │
│   Thickened                │
│   Lightened                │
│   Skewed                   │
│   Underlined               │
│                            │
└────────────────────────────┘
```

```
┌────────────────┐
│ Colours        │
├────────────────┤
│ Colours        │
│ 0 — 15         │   For text and graphics
│ Graphics       │
│ 0 — 15         │   Can be chosen independently
│                │
└────────────────┘
```

Patterns	
0 − 38	Choice of patterns to fill shapes

Lines	
1 − 6	Line styles
1 , 3 , 5 , 7	Line thicknesses
0 − 2	Left hand line ends
0 − 2	Right hand line ends

Windows
Show Results-1
Hide Results-1
****
Show Results-2
Hide Results-2
****
Show Edit
Hide Edit
****
Show Dialogue
Hide Dialogue

Move the pointer to **BASIC2** and a further menu is displayed:

```
About BASIC2...

Calculator
Clock
Print Spooler
```

where the first option gives the version number of BASIC2 in use. The latest version available is 1.14 at the time of writing.

If you move the arrow to the **WINDOWS** command the pull-down menu gives the choice of displaying or hiding any of the windows. This will avoid the possibility of cluttering up the screen with windows you do not require at the time.

In order to run a program you move the arrow to the **FILE** command at the top of the screen and select **RUN**.

The function keys (F1 – F10) on the left of the keyboard have specific functions in BASIC2; they are mentioned on the pulldown menus as well:

F1   Marks the start or finish of a block of program.
F2   Stops marking a section of program.
F3   Inserts marked section at cursor position.
F4   Moves marked section to cursor position.
F5   Removes marked section.
F7   Restarts a stopped program.
F9   Runs the current program.
F10 Goes into EDIT mode.

The main commands in BASIC2

In the version of BASIC supplied with the Amstrad PC1512 variable names can be of any length of which the first 40 characters are significant. A variable cannot bear a name which is one of the BASIC keywords as listed in the following pages. Variable names can be entered in either upper or lower case, but will always be displayed in lower case. Spaces are not allowed but you can separate words within a variable name by the underline character. Valid names are

g   a0   best_buy   sum_of_costs

Variable types are:

String variables   names which terminate in a $ sign. Can contain anything from zero (null string) to 255 characters.

t$ john$ a0$ company$

Arrays of numerics or strings   must include subscripts in parentheses.

a$(3,4)   total(4)   number(j,k,l)

Hexadecimal numbers   have the prefix &.

&FFF   &100   &001

Binary numbers   have the prefix &X.

&X001   &X01010   &X111111111

Storage classes

You can define the way in which numbers are stored by BASIC2 by specifiying a *storage class*. There are five storage classes each of which take differing amounts of memory. They are:

BYTE   UBYTE   WORD   UWORD   INTEGER

BYTE and UBYTE take up one byte of storage. WORD and UWORD take up two bytes of storage and INTEGER takes up four bytes.

Numbers in the range −128 to 127 can be stored in the BYTE class. Numbers in the range 0 to 255 can be stored in the the UBYTE class. WORD and UWORD numbers can be in the range −32768 to 32767 and 0 to 65535 respectively. INTEGERs can be in the range −2147483648 to 2147483647.

The class can be defined after a DIM statement so that you can write

DIM table(200,200) UBYTE

providing you only intend to use numbers in the allowable range.

Space can be allotted to the elements of string arrays, but in a different way. It is done by defining the maximum length of each string element in bytes (characters). For example

DIM home$(500) FIXED 50

ensuring that no entry in the array will take up more than 50 bytes of storage.

The class definition is also used when index keys are defined for keyed access files.

Order of execution of BASIC2 arithmetic

1. Brackets
2. Unary + and −
3. Exponentiation, ^, sign
4. Multiplication and division, / sign, Integer division, \
   sign, MOD
5. Addition and subtraction

Operations in parentheses are performed first. Equal
precedence operations are performed from left to
right.

One important difference between this version of
the BASIC language and those available on other PCs
is that the usual line numbers are not necessary. If you
want to use line numbers then the only numbers that
are needed are those that are used as labels for lines
referenced by GOTO or GOSUB instructions. Even
line numbers for this purpose are not necessary since
BASIC2 allows you to use labels to mark sections of
the program. You can see how these work if you look
at the description of the LABEL command in the
section following. The lines of BASIC2 instructions are
executed in the order of their appearance and so extra
lines have to be inserted by editing.

To enter a BASIC2 program move into the EDIT
window from the DIALOGUE window by pressing the
F10 key. Then you can enter your program instructions
line by line. To run the program press the F9 key. You
should note that BASIC2, unlike other versions of the
language, has no such thing as a 'direct' mode,
because of the lack of line numbers. Every program,
even a one-liner, must be run by pressing the F9 key.

You can edit programs in the EDIT window by making sure that the INS key has been pressed so that you can enter a new line of program between two existing lines. You can do this by moving the mouse pointer to the appropriate line and clicking it. Press the ENTER key and a new blank line will open up for you. Then you can enter your new line. To delete a line move the pointer to the line to be deleted and click. Then press the DEL key and you will be able to delete the line one character at a time.

BASIC2 statements
In the following examples many of the BASIC2 statements given are followed by a single quote mark (') this is the equivalent of the word REM (REMark) which is a comment entered for explanatory purposes only.

ABS returns the absolute value of a numeric expression.

```
x=2.3:x1=−1
y=ABS(x)
z=ABS(x∗x1) :'Stores 2.3 in both x and y
```

ADDKEY is used with keyed random access files to add a new key for an existing record.

ADDREC adds a new record and its key to a keyed random access file.

ALERT displays an 'Alert Box' on the screen.

ASC returns the ASCII code for the first character of a string.

```
x$="BILL"
x=ASC(x$) :'Stores 66 in x
```

ATAN returns the arctangent (in radians unless degrees have been chosen by OPTION DEGREES) of a numeric expression. Can be abbreviated to ATN.

```
p=3.09
q=ATAN(p):'Stores 1.25780894 in q
```

Similarly ASIN and ACOS will return arcsine and arccosine.

ATAN2 is used to convert Cartesian (x,y) coordinates to Polar (r,θ) coordinates.

```
a = ATAN2(p,q) :'Will provide the angle (A) in a
right angled triangle with opposite and adjacent
sides of length p and q.
```

BIN$ will return a string of binary digits equivalent to the integer argument. For example

```
b$ = BIN$(12)
```

will place the string "1100" in the variable called **b$**.

CEILING will round its argument to an integer towards + infinity so that

```
CEILING(−9.9)
```

will return −9.

CHDIR has the same effect as in DOS, that is to change from the current directory to another. Can be abbreviated to CD as in DOS.

CHDIR$ will return the name of the current directory in use.

CHDIR(\WP) will change the current directory to one called WP.

CLEAR will reset all variables to zeros or nulls and close all open files.

CLS will clear a specified window. For example

CLS #2 will clear a window that has been defined by an OPEN WINDOW command.

CLS RESET will restore a text style to its original state and then clear the screen.

COLOUR will specify the colour of text or graphics displayed in a particular window.

PRINT#2, COLOUR(4);"HERE WE ARE AGAIN"

will print the words in quotes in the Results-2 window in colour 4.

CHR$ returns the character represented by the ASCII decimal code specified in the argument.

PRINT CHR$(66):'Will print the character "B"

CINT returns the integer value of a numeric expression by rounding. Works almost exactly the same as the ROUND function.

    PRINT CINT(3.456):'Prints the number 3
    PRINT CINT(−3.456):'Prints the number −3
    PRINT CINT(−2.9):'Prints −3

CLOSE closes any input/output device or file previously OPENed.

    CLOSE#1 :'Closes file on Stream 1.
    CLOSE :'Closes all open files.

CONT resumes execution of the program after the program has been interrupted by CONTROL-C, END or STOP instructions in the program. If the program has been edited after it stopped you will get the "Can't continue" message.

COS is the trigonometric cosine of the argument (which must be in radians, unless OPTION DEGREES has been selected).

    x=3.141593
    c=COS(x) Stores the number −1 in c.

DATA must prefix a data list accessed by a READ statement.

    DATA 100,"10,Mornington Crescent",Harry,&00FA

DATE$ is an 8 character string variable of the form DD/MM/YY.It may have been set by the operating system prior to use of BASIC2.

    PRINT DATE$ 'Will print, for example, "31/01/87"

DATE$(1000) will give the date 1000 days after 31st December 1899.

DATE gives the number of days since 31st December 1899.

DATE(DD/MM/YY) will return the number of days from 31st December 1899 to the date string entered as the argument.

DEC$ will return a formatted decimal string from a given decimal number. The template used is the same as is used in a PRINT USING instruction. For example:

```
PRINT DEC$(1489.5, ###,###.##)
```

will return

```
1,489.50
```

DEF FN defines a function used within the program. FN is followed by a name for the function and by its definition.

```
DEF FNcash(p,t,r)=p*t*r/100
INPUT principal,years,rate
interest=FNcash(principal,years,rate)
PRINT interest
```

Note: Do not use a variable called **time** as this is a reserved name in BASIC2.

DEG will convert an angle from radians to degrees.

DEL has the same effect as the DOS command of the same name. It will delete a named file. Wildcards can be used in the file name specified after the command.

DELKEY will delete a key from the index file associated with a keyed random access file.

DIM defines the range of array subscripts.

DIM a(100,100),size$(150),pos(x,y,z)

When the DIM command is used the first element in the array is numbered 0. If you wish to specify the range of numbered elements then the command must be of the form

DIM a(1 TO 50)

Where the elements are numbered from 1 to 50.

DIMENSIONS will return the number of dimensions of an array. For example

DIMENSIONS(size$())

will return the number 150.

DIR has the same effect as the command of the same name in DOS. It will list the files stored in the current directory.

DISPLAY will show the contents of a text file. The command

DISPLAY #3, filename

will display the contents of the named file on Stream 3. The stream number is not essential, but the file must be a text file.

DRIVE will set the default drive.

DRIVE ("B:") will set the default drive to drive B:.

END will stop a program.

    END :'Does not have to be the last program
    statement

EOF refers to an end of file marker. If an end of file
marker is found then EOF is set to 'True' , i.e. -1.
Otherwise it is set to 'False', i.e. 0. Only relevant to
serial files.

    LABEL test
    IF EOF(#1) THEN GOTO end
    INPUT #1,a,b,c
    PRINT a,b,c
    GOTO test :'Note how this takes you to the EOF
                test and then the next file input
                statement, not the other way round
    LABEL end
    END

ERASE has the same effect as the command of the
same name in DOS. It will erase one or more named
files.

    ERASE ("*.BAK") will erase all files in the current
    directory with a .BAK extension.

ERR is the numerical error code for the last error
encountered. Using the ON ERROR command:

```
ON ERROR GOTO fault
INPUT "Name:"; name$
IF name$="Fred" THEN GOTO fred ELSE
   GOTO other
LABEL fred
PRINT "Hello Fred!"
STOP
LABEL fault
IF ERR=20 THEN PRINT ERROR$(20)
STOP
```

ERROR$ will return the error message associated with
the error number specified (see below).

ERROR$(20) will display the error message for error
number 20, which is that a label does not exist

EXP returns the exponential function.

```
x=2.4
PRINT EXP(x) :'Prints 11.02318
```

FILES lists the filenames of those files, program or
data, which are stored on disk.

```
FILES :'Lists all files present
FILES ("*.DAT") :'Lists all files with .DAT extension
```

Uses wildcards in the same way as DOS.

FINDDIR$ will search the current drive to find a directory matching that specified. So that

    answer$ = FINDDIR$("sale*")

will store the name of the first directory on the current disk starting with the characters **sale**.

FIX has the same effect as the TRUNC function. It rounds a number towards zero.

FLOOR will round a number to the next smallest whole number. Has the same effect as the INT function.

FOR/NEXT sets up a program loop defining the number of times the instructions in the loop are to be executed.

    FOR start_value of variable TO target_value STEP increment
      body of loop
    NEXT variable

If the increment is omitted it is taken to be 1.

    FOR i=1 TO 10 STEP 0.5
    PRINT i^2 :'Prints the values of 1^2,1.5^2,2^2...10^2
    NEXT i

The variable specified in NEXT can be omitted if it is unambiguous. FOR/NEXT loops can be nested one within another.

You can test how a FOR/NEXT works by running the following program:

```
INPUT start,finish,increment
'Use test values of 1,10,1 then 1,1,1 and then 2,1,1
FOR value=start TO finish STEP increment
PRINT value;
NEXT
PRINT "FINAL VALUE ";value
```

FRAC returns the fractional part of a number.

```
x=FRAC(y) :'Assigns the fractional part of the
number stored in y to the variable x.
```

FRE returns the number of bytes of memory available to your program at that point. All the spare string space is collected up into useful string space. For example the command

```
PRINT FRE
```

will display the number of bytes of free memory, and 'garbage collection' will have taken place as well.

GET gets a specified record from a random or a keyed index file and places it into the buffer.

```
GET #6, data$ AT 15 :'Gets the string data$ from
the 15th record of file #6. If the record number is
omitted the current record is read. (See example of
a simple random file at the end of this section.)
```

GOSUB/RETURN interrupts program flow to execute a subroutine at a specified line number and on encountering RETURN jumps back to the statement following the original GOSUB.

```
GOSUB rest
STOP :'Rest of program would be here
LABEL rest
PRINT "HERE WE ARE"
RETURN
```

GOTO is an unconditional jump statement to cause execution to be transferred to the instructions starting at the specified line number or label.

```
GOTO 1000 :'Next instruction executed is on line
1000
```

```
GOTO Compute :'The next instruction executed
follows the label Compute
```

HEX$ returns the hexadecimal value of a decimal number in string form.

```
x=100
H$=HEX$(x) :'Sets H$ to be "64"
```

IF/THEN/ELSE allows conditional branching to take place on the result of evaluating the truth or otherwise of the IF statement.

```
INPUT number
IF number<10 THEN PRINT "SMALL" ELSE PRINT
"LARGE"
```

The instruction following the THEN and the ELSE can be any valid BASIC2 instruction. Beware of an IF statement which looks like this:

    IF 1<number<10 THEN PRINT "IN RANGE"

The ELSE clause is optional. IF statements can be used in conjunction with AND, OR and NOT conjunctions. For example:

    IF number<10 AND number>1 THEN PRINT "IN RANGE"
    IF number>10 OR number<1 THEN PRINT "OUT OF RANGE"

An expression such as

    IF k THEN GOTO true

tests to see if k is zero or non-zero. Only if k is non-zero (true) then the jump to the line labelled 'true' is made. The truth or otherwise of a statement is determined by the values of the *logical* operators in the program. A value of 0 indicates a false condition whereas a non-zero value indicates truth.

Try this simple program to see how it works:

    FOR k=-3 TO 3
    IF k THEN PRINT k;" TRUE" ELSE PRINT k;" FALSE"
    NEXT k

Similarly

    IF NOT k THEN GOTO untrue

will only jump to the line labelled **untrue** if NOT(k) is true, i.e. if **k** has any value such that NOT k is non-zero.

This program illustrates how this works:

```
FOR k=-3 TO 3
IF NOT k THEN PRINT k:" TRUE" ELSE PRINT k;
   "FALSE"
NEXT k
```

If both operands are 0 or −1 then the logical operators return 0 or −1, i.e. NOT(0) is −1 and NOT(−1) is 0.

INKEY\$ reads one character from the keyboard. A program segment which waits for any key to be pressed before carrying on is:

```
LABEL inkey
kb$=INKEY$
IF kb$="" THEN GOTO inkey
```

Or if you want to wait for a specific key to be pressed:

```
LABEL inkey
kb$=INKEY$
IF kb$="" THEN GOTO inkey
IF kb$<>"B" THEN GOTO inkey
```

INKEY\$ does not require the ENTER key to be pressed.

INKEY works in a similar manner to INKEY\$ but returns −1 if no key has been depressed. When a key is pressed that key's ASCII code is returned.

INPUT stores the input from the keyboard in a list of named variables.

```
INPUT x,y,a$
```

A prompt string can be included in the statement:

```
INPUT "Type in your name ";name$
```

INPUT # reads data from a device or a file and stores the data in specified program variables. The file must have been OPENed in the correct mode for this to take place.

```
INPUT #2,a,b,c$
```

INPUT$ is similar to INKEY$ in that the keyboard response is not echoed and RETURN is not needed. It can be used for accepting only certain characters as input:

```
LABEL start
PRINT "TYPE IN THE PASSWORD"
x$=INPUT$(6)
'The argument is the number of characters
   accepted
IF x$="SNOOPY" THEN GOTO finish ELSE GOTO
   start
```

Input can be accepted from a specified file if its channel number is specified and the file has already been opened in the correct mode.

```
s$=INPUT$ (#1,6)
```

INSTR will determine where a particular string exists within a specified string of characters.

```
INSTR(1,word$,"ie")
```

If the string of characters "ie" is contained in **word$** then the function returns the position in the string of the specified characters.

KEY or KEY$ set the position of the index on the index file associated with a keyed randon access file. KEY is for a numeric key and KEY$ for a character key. If you wish to determine the key corresponding to the current pointer position then you can code it as

    k=KEY (#2)

or

    k$=KEY$ (#4)

depending on whether the key is numerical or a string.

KEYSPEC defines the index file to hold the index to a keyed random access file.

    KEYSPEC #2, INDEX FIXED 6 specifies that the key to the file in stream 2 is of a fixed length of 6. The type specified after the word INDEX can be one of BYTE, UBYTE, WORD, UWORD, INTEGER or FIXED.

KILL deletes a named file from disk.

    KILL ("PROG1")
    KILL "(A:DATA1") :'Deletes file "DATA1" from the disk in drive A

LABEL prefixes a label within the program.

    LABEL input1
    INPUT "Type in a number";number

    IF number=0 GOTO input1

Or you can use the label to mark a subroutine.

```
GOSUB message
---
---
LABEL message
PRINT #2; COLOUR(4); "Have a nice day!"
RETURN
```

LEFT$ locates the leftmost n characters of a string.

```
bit$=LEFT(string$,10) :'Stores the first ten
characters of string$ in bit$
```

LEN returns the length of (i.e. number of characters in) a string.

```
length = LEN(string$) :'Stores the number of
characters in string$ in length
```

LINE INPUT and LINE INPUT# read a string containing commas into a variable or a file record.

```
LINE INPUT address$ :'Would read a string such as
"17,Main St" into address$
```

```
LINE INPUT #2,address$ :'Would read "17,Main
St" into next record of serial file #2
```

LOCATE Will move the cursor to a specified row and column of a virtual screen. For example

```
LOCATE #2,10;45
```

will move the cursor on virtual screen 2 to row 10, column 45.

LOC returns current position of the file pointer. It is the record number of the last record read from a random file or the number of records read so far from a serial file.

IF LOC #2 = 75 THEN GOSUB subr1 :'Tests to see if it has read the 75th record from the file

LOF returns the length of a file in bytes.

n=LOF (#4) :'Stores number of bytes taken up by file 4 in **n**

LOG returns the natural logarithm of the argument.

x = 3.4 : y=LOG(x) :'Stores 1.22377543 in **y**

LOG10 returns the logarithm to the base 10 of the argument.

LOWER will return the lower bound of an array dimension.

LOWER$ converts a string to lower case.

word$ = LOWER$("CAMBRIDGE") will store the string "cambridge" in **word$**.

LPRINT and LPRINT USING directs the output to the printer instead of the screen.

LPRINT "The total is :";total

LSET left justifies a string in the field occupied by another string variable.

name$="PETER":LSET a$=name$

60

MID$ returns a portion of a specified string.

    bit$=MID$(string$,4,2) :'Stores the substring of
    string$ which is two characters long, starting with the
    fourth character, in **bit$**

MOD returns the remainder after one number is
divided by another. For example the number stored in
remainder after the instruction

    remainder = 15 MOD 4

will be 3.

NAME allows a file stored on disk to be renamed so
that the instruction

    NAME ("oldfile") AS ("newfile")

will change the name of the file **oldfile** to become
newfile.

NEW deletes the program currently in memory.

ON ERROR, ON/GOSUB, ON/GOTO direct program
flow to specified lines of BASIC2 program depending
on certain conditions being fulfilled.

    ON ERROR GOTO 500 :'If an error condition
                               occurs, go to line 500
    ON k GOTO 200,300,400 :'If k = 1 goto line 200,
    if k = 2 goto line 300, if k = 3 go to line 400.
    Otherwise go to next statement

    ON j GOSUB 600,700,800
    'As above but subroutines executed

OPEN opens a channel to or from a file on the current backing store.

OPEN #2 INPUT "stockfile"

where the mode, placed after the stream number, is OUTPUT,INPUT or APPEND (disk files only). Between the stream number and the mode the keywords NEW or OLD can be inserted, for OUTPUT and APPEND only. If NEW is used a new file of the specified filename is created. If OLD is used then the command ensures that the file does really exist.

Use of an OPEN command such as

OPEN #3 RANDOM "b:birthdays"

will open a random access file on Stream 3 called **birthdays** on drive B. Again NEW or OLD can precede the RANDOM keyword. The record length can also be specified at the end of the command so that you could write

OPEN #4 NEW RANDOM "houses" LENGTH 50

to open a new random access file called **houses** where each record is to be 50 characters long.

You should notice that with these commands there are no commas, only spaces, separating the parameters. This is quite unlike the other versions of the BASIC language. (See the end of this section for simple examples of sequential and random file handling.)

PI will return the numerical value of the Greek letter pi.

POS returns the current column of the cursor.

```
IF POS(0)>70 THEN CHR$(13) :'Issues the
'carriage return' code when the cursor passes
column 70
```

POSITION or POSITION$ return the position of the
current index in the index file associated with a keyed
random access file. POSITION is for numeric keys and
POSITION$ for character keys.

PRINT or PRINT USING output data to the screen.

```
PRINT #1 will direct the output to Results Screen
#1
```

and

```
PRINT #2 will direct the output to Results Screen
#2.
```

```
PRINT #2 "HELLO SAILOR!"
p=23.45
PRINT #2, USING "###.####";p :'Prints 23.4500
```

PRINT # and PRINT #, USING act as above but print
to a specified file, which must have been OPENed.

```
PRINT #2,a$,b$
PRINT #3,USING "###.####";p
```

PUT places the contents of the random file buffer in the specified record of the file. For example the instruction

    PUT #5,LSET(name$) AT 1

places the variable named into the first record on the random access file opened on Stream 5. (See example of a simple random access file at the end of this section.)

Note: The Locomotive BASIC2 Manual is in error on this – they leave the AT out.

QUIT exits BASIC2 and returns you to DOS. The same as the SYSTEM command.

RANDOMIZE sets the random number generator going. It can be 'seeded' with a numerical value. Otherwise it takes its starting value from the PC's internal clock.

    RANDOMIZE (660)

READ reads values, numeric or string, from a DATA line.

    READ a$,b,c$

RECORD will define a record structure for a random access file. Data can only be stored in character format in a random access file. It is defined by using this instruction and listing the 'name' of the record and the fields it contains

    RECORD record; stockno INTEGER, descrip$
    FIXED 12

where the variable **record** defines the record structure. The description of each field then follows.

REM is the remark statement ignored by the BASIC2 interpreter. Can be replaced by a single quote symbol. REM statements can be branched to.

    REM THIS IS A REMARK
    'SO IS THIS

REN has the same effect as the command of the same name in DOS. It will rename a file.

    REN file1 file2
    'Renames the file called **file1** as **file2**

   Note that REN does not need the names included between brackets and surrounded by quotation marks as does the NAME command.

REPEAT sets up a loop of instructions that are executed UNTIL a particular condition is fulfilled. A simple use of the construction is shown below. You should compare it with the WHILE and WEND construction.

```
sum + 0
REPEAT
INPUT NUMBER
sum = sum + number
UNTIL sum>50
PRINT sum
```

REPOSITION will alter the position of the record pointer in a file. For example

```
REPOSITION #2, 200
```

will move the pointer to the 200th record on another file on Stream 2.

RESTORE returns the pointer after reading from a DATA line, to an earlier line number allowing the data to be reread.

```
RESTORE 300 :'Returns the pointer to line 300
```

The default value is the first line of DATA.

RESUME resumes program execution after an error recovery has taken place.

```
RESUME 0 'Resumes at line where error occurred.
The 0 is optional
RESUME NEXT :'Resumes at line after the error
RESUME 190 :'Resumes at line 190
```

RETURN transfers control from a subroutine to the instruction following the GOSUB instruction.

```
5000:'SUBROUTINE STARTS HERE
RETURN :'RETURNS CONTROL TO MAIN
PROGRAM
```

RIGHT$ returns the rightmost n characters from a string.

```
bit$=RIGHT$(string$,5)
'Stores the rightmost 5 characters of string$ in bit$
```

RAD will convert an angle in degrees into radians.

RND returns a random number in the range 0 to 1. To generate random integers in the range 0 through n you need INT(RND$\star$(n+1)).

RMDIR works exactly the same as the command in DOS. It removes a directory. An alternative command is RD.

ROUND will round a decimal number to a specified number of decimal places. For example

```
ROUND(number,3)
```

will round the contents of the variable **number** to three places of decimals.

RSET acts like LSET but right-justifies in the buffer field.

SCREEN will define a virtual screen. The choices are:

SCREEN #3 GRAPHICS

to define a virtual screen as a graphics screen.

SCREEN #2 TEXT

to define a virtual screen as a text screen.

SCREEN #5 TEXT FLEXIBLE

to define a text screen with a width equal to the window.

Further parameters can define the sizes of the screen.

SGN returns the sign ($+$ or $-$) of the argument. If positive, 1 is returned. If negative then -1 is returned and if zero, 0 is returned.

```
p=-10
k=SGN(p) :'Stores -1 in k
```

SIN is the trigonometric sign function. The argument will normally be in radians, not degrees. This can be changed by the OPTION DEGREES command.

```
x=1.2
s=SIN(x) :'Stores .9320391 in s
```

SQR evaluates the square root of the argument.

```
x=45.78
y=SQR(x) :'Stores 6.766092 in y
```

STOP terminates the execution of your program. You can continue with CONT.

STR$ assigns the string representation of a numeric variable to a string variable.

```
x=5.78
x$=STR$(x) :'Stores "5.78" in x$
```

STRING$ produces a string of n specified characters.

```
string$=STRING$(10,"*") :'Stores a string of 10
```
"*" characters in **string$**

SWAP will exchange the values of two variables.

SWAP p,q :'Exchanges the values of p and q and is the equivalent of:

```
t=p:p=q:q=t
```

SYSTEM returns you from BASIC2 to DOS. Identical to QUIT.

TAB tabs printer or screen cursor n spaces.

```
PRINT TAB(25);"HELLO"
'Prints the characters starting in the 25th column
```

TAN gives the trigonometric tangent of the argument, which will usually be in radians. This can be changed by using the OPTION DEGREES command.

```
x=0.5
tan=TAN(0.5) :'Stores 0.5463025 in tan
```

TIME returns the time since midnight in hundredths of a second. The time may have been set from within DOS and can be accessed from BASIC2, as with DATE$.

TRUNC has the same effect as FIX.

TYPE has the same effect as the DOS command of the same name. It will display the contents of a named text file. Be careful, however, that you do not try to TYPE a binary file. If you do it can have a disastrous effect on the screen display.

UPPER returns the upper dimension of an array.

UPPER$ converts a character string into upper case.

```
string$="aeiou"
text$=UPPER$(string$)
PRINT text$
```

will result in the characters "AEIOU" being displayed.

VAL converts a string variable into its numerical equivalent. If the first character of the string is non-numeric, 0 is returned.

```
v=VAL("567.8") :'Stores 567.8 in v
```

VPOS returns the current line of the cursor on the screen.

WHILE/WEND is a looping instruction executed 'while' a condition holds. You should compare this with the REPEAT UNTIL construction.

```
reply$="YES"            Note that the value of R$
WHILE reply$="YES"      has to be "seeded" with
INPUT number            "YES" otherwise the loop
total=total+number      will never be entered at all
INPUT reply$
WEND
PRINT total
```

WHOLE$ returns the whole of a fixed length string
including any nulls.

Simple file handling

1 Sequential file: This program is in two parts. In the
first part ten strings are written to sequential records of
a file. The second part of the program reads the
records in sequence and displays them on the screen

```
file = 6
OPEN #file OUTPUT "b:names"
FOR i = 1 TO 10
INPUT "Word";a$
PRINT #file, a$
NEXT
CLOSE #file
OPEN #file INPUT "b:names"
FOR i = 1 TO 10
INPUT #file, c$
PRINT c$
NEXT
CLOSE #file
```

2 Random access file: This example opens a random access file, writes five records to it and then allows you to read back the contents of those records in any order you wish.

```
RECORD rec; n$ FIXED 4
OPEN #4 RANDOM "b:rfile"
FOR i = 1 TO 5
INPUT "Record ";recno
INPUT "Data";number
n$=STR$(number)
PUT #4, n$ AT recno
NEXT
LABEL more
INPUT "Find record ";n
IF n=0 THEN GOTO finish
GET #4, n$ AT n
PRINT n$
GOTO more
LABEL finish
CLOSE #4
```

User Options
BASIC2 offers a series of OPTIONS to the user, these are:

OPTION CURRENCY$ to set the appropriate currency symbol.

OPTION DATE to define the format of a date string.

OPTION DECIMAL to set the style of the decimal point and the thousands separator when PRINT USING commands are used.

OPTION DEGREES to force all trigonometrical evaluations to be in degrees rather than radians.

OPTION INKEY$ to set translations for special keys in conjunction with INKEY$.

OPTION RADIANS to force all angles to be expressed in radians rather than degrees.

OPTION RUN to prevent a BASIC2 program from being stopped – by the use of Control-C – during running.

OPTION SELFILE$ to set the parameters of file selectors.

OPTION SELPATH$ to set the parameters of path selectors.

OPTION SELWILD$ to set the parameters of wildcard selectors.

OPTION STOP to undo the OPTION RUN command.

OPTION TRAP to turn off, or on, the trapping of undefined values.

GEM control commands
There are a number of special commands that control GEM from within a BASIC2 program. They are:

XPOS, YPOS define the current cursor position.

XMOUSE, YMOUSE define the current mouse position on the real screen (in pixels).

XWINDOW, YWINDOW define the size of the current window (in pixels).

XSCROLL, YSCROLL define the coordinates of the window on the virtual screen.

XPLACE, YPLACE define the coordinates of the window on the screen (in pixels).

USER SPACE defines the size of the virtual screen used for graphics.

WINDOW OPEN/CLOSE opens up or hides a window.

WINDOW PLACE sets the place of a window on the screen (measured in pixels).

WINDOW SCROLL scrolls a window over its virtual screen to set to a specified point.

WINDOW SIZE defines the dimensions of a window.

WINDOW TITLE specifies the title to be displayed in a window.

WINDOW CURSOR will hide/display the cursor in a given window.

WINDOW INFORMATION will display specified text on the window information line.

WINDOW FULL will make a window its full size, or reduce it from full size.

WINDOW MOUSE will alter the form of the mouse pointer in a window.

XDEVICE, YDEVICE, XMETRES, YMETRES define the dimensions of a screen in pixels and metres respectively.

XACTUAL, YACTUAL, XWINDOW, YWINDOW define
the width and height of a window (in pixels).

XVIRTUAL. YVIRTUAL define the dimensions of a
graphics screen.

XCELL, YCELL, XPIXEL, YPIXEL Define the sizes of
screen characters and picture cells (pixels).

XBAR, YBAR define the width and height of the
window border (in pixels).

YASPECT will return the aspect ratio (ratio of width to
height) of a window.

XUSABLE, YUSABLE will return the usable width and
height of a screen (in pixels).

Graphics and other special commands in BASIC2
BASIC2 divides your screen up into a grid of 5000 by
5000 units and all distances and coordinates are
referred to these. Fuller descriptions of the detailed
use of these commands can be found in the
Locomotive BASIC2 User Guide.

ARC draws the arc of a circle through a pair of
specified points

    ARC A;B,C;D

where A;B and C;D are the coordinates of the pair of
points. (*Note:* the manual supplied with your Amstrad
PC mentions an ARC function. However, in the
Locomotive BASIC2 Manual this function is not listed
and another way of drawing an arc is given. This also
applies to elliptical arcs).

BOX draws a rectangle where the coordinates of its lower left hand corner, its width (W) and its height (H) are defined in the command.

BOX X;Y,W,H

is the general form of the command. You should note that coordinates are separated by a semi-colon (;) while the rest of the parameters are separated by commas.

CIRCLE actually draws an ellipse on the screen. Parameters are the coordinates of the centre and the radius. The command is

CIRCLE X;Y,R

where X and Y are the coordinates of the centre and R is the radius. An example would be

CIRCLE 1000;1000,500

where the circle would be drawn at coordinates 1000, 1000 and the radius would be 500 units.

CIRCLE X;Y, R PART A1,A2

where A1 and A2 are the starting and finishing angles of the arc in radians or degrees depending on which have been chosen by OPTION DEGREES.

ELLIPSE will draw an ellipse whose centre is at a specified point and whose radius (R) and aspect ratio (A) are defined. The aspect ratio ensures that the semi-minor axis is determined by multiplying the semi-major axis by the aspect ratio.

ELLIPSE X;Y,R,A

ELLIPSE X;Y,R,A PART A1,A2

will draw an elliptical arc between the two angles A1 and A2.

ELLIPTICAL ARC plots an elliptical arc between points A,B and C,D with radius R with aspect ratio (A).

ELLIPTICAL ARC A;B,C;D,R,A (*Note:* the same comment applies as with the drawing of a circular arc).

ELLIPTICAL PIE plots an elliptical 'pie slice' with a centre at X,Y, radius R, aspect ratio A and between angles A1 and A2

ELLIPTICAL PIE X;Y,R,A,A1,A2

LINE draws straight lines through specified points. The form of the command is

LINE A;B,C;D,E;F.......

where A;B are the coordinates of the first point, C;D are the coordinates of the second point and so on.

PIE draws a 'pie slice' of a specified radius (R) with a defined centre (X,Y) between two specified arcs (A1 and A2).

PIE X;Y,R,A1,A2

PLOT plots a list of points each defined by its coordinates.

PLOT A;B,C;D,E;F.....

SHAPE draws a polygon with vertices at the points specified in the list

SHAPE A;B,C;D,E;F,G;H.......

Most of these commands can be modified by a series of additonal commands such as

FILL WITH 3 STYLE 5

to fill the area plotted with a particular colour or pattern and to draw the outline with a particular style of line.

In addition there are what are known as *Turtle graphics* in which a pointer, known as a 'turtle', can be moved about the screen in order to draw shapes. The commands that control the turtle are

GRAPHICS CURSOR 3 will set the cursor up as the turtle ready to be moved about. Initially this is pointed horizontally to the right.

DISTANCE (X;Y) which is the distance of the point with coordinates X,Y from the current turtle position.

FD or FORWARD **d**, where **d** is a distance, moves the turtle in the direction of the point of the arrow without drawing a line.

HEADING is the current turtle angle.

LEFT or LT **angle** turns the turtle to the left through the specified angle.

MOVE FD or MOVE FORWARD **d** will draw a line as the turtle moves.

POINT turns the turtle to point in a specified direction.

RIGHT or RT **angle** turns the turtle to the right through the specified angle.

4 DOSplus Version 1.2 and GEM Paint

DOSPlus enables you to run many MS-DOS programs together with programs written to run under the CP/M86 operating system.

Internal DOSPlus commands
The internal DOSPlus operating system commands are nearly all the same as those for MS-DOS 3.2 and they operate in the same manner, although the output they produce is displayed slightly differently. You can check their syntax by referring to the first section of this Handbook. These commands are:

CHDIR	FOR	REM
CLS	GOTO	RMDIR
COPY	IF	SET
DATE	MKDIR	SHIFT
DIR	PATH	TIME
ECHO	PAUSE	

There are other internal commands specific to DOSPlus, which are:

ADDMEM which allocates additional memory for programs with a .EXE extension. The command ADDMEM on its own will tell you how much memory is allocated.

COMSIZE sets the memory size for .COM programs. The command on its own returns the size of memory allocated.

DELQ which deletes one or more files from the disk.

ERAQ works in the same manner as DELQ.

SLICE allocates a slice of processing time to foreground programs. SLICE on its own returns the size of this time slice.

External DOSPlus commands
ALARM which sets up a list of dates and times with messages to be displayed at required times. The command consists of ALARM followed by the date and the time of the alarm, in the approved format, followed by the message. This message will be displayed when the date and time have been been reached on the PCs internal clock. The display is accompanied by a short musical phrase to draw your attention to it.

BACKG lists the programs running in the background.

DEVICE will list the status of the devices attached to your PC. DEVICE will also allow you to change the status of any device, i.e. the baud rate of a communication port.

DISK is a utility that enables you to copy the contents of one diskette to another, format a diskette and verify that files on a diskette have been copied accurately.

FSET sets label and drive attributes.

N allows you to select the language in which you want your keyboard to be configured and the printer to which your PC is connected.

PIP is the equivalent of COPY. PIP actually stands for Peripheral Interchange Program and allows files to be moved about from disk to disk or device to device. The important feature of PIP that you should notice is that the order of copying is the reverse of that in COPY. The command takes the form of

    PIP <target filename>=<source filename>

so that

    PIP B:SALESA=A:SALES1

will copy the file called SALES1 on drive A onto the disk in drive B and give the copied file the name SALESA.

  If you wish to copy a large number of files you can issue the PIP command, which responds with the ∗ symbol, and then you can enter the PIPping commands one at a time. You leave PIP by pressing the Return (Enter) key.

PRINT sets up a queue of files to be printed in the background while foreground processing continues.

RPED is a full screen editor that enables you to edit files up to 750 lines long.

SHOW provides you with details of various features of your system. For example,

SHOW [SPACE]

gives you the amount of free space available on the disks mounted in your disk drives.

SHOW [DRIVE]

gives the drive characteristics.

SHOW B:[DIR]

gives you the number of free directory entries on drive B.

SHOW [LABEL]

gives you the label information for the disk in the current drive.

TREE has the same effect as the similar command in MS-DOS

GEM Paint

In order to run GEM Paint you need to create a special GEM Paint disk using programs that are supplied on both the MS-DOS disk and the DOSPlus disk. A full description of how this is done is given in the handbook supplied with your PC1512.

Once this has been done, and it is rather a lengthy task, you get into GEM Paint from the Desktop in conjunction with your newly created Paint disk.

You select the PAINT.APP icon from the Desktop and double click the mouse. The new screen is your 'paper' and 'paintbox'. The menu list displayed at the top of the screen contains

File Tools Selection Patterns Font Style   PAINT

The File menu offers the same options as the menu displayed when you are running BASIC2.

The Tools menu allows you to select the shape of the 'brush' or 'spray' you are going to use to create your picture. In addition you can define the size of the painting surface, erase parts of your picture and place text within the picture.

Patterns, Font and Style offer you choices for the details of your picture. The Selector menu provides the ability to copy selected areas of the screen into other parts of the screen.

WordStar 1512

Despite its name the only relationship that this wordprocessor, specifically designed for use with your Amstrad PC1512, has with the well-known wordprocessor of the same name is the fact that its file structure is compatible with both the common WordStar and WordStar 2000 wordprocessors. It is the first, and potentially the most common, piece of software designed for use on this machine and it is for this reason that a description of its features has been included in this Handbook. WordStar 1512 is in fact marketed by Amstrad rather than MicroPro, the company who produce the WordStar, WordStar 2000 and WordStar Professional wordprocessors.

This single package contains all the expected wordprocessor features together with the CorrectStar spelling checker (in English, not American) and a mail-merge feature. The data files associated with this feature can be used as a rudimentary database. It is *menu-driven* from a series of pull-down menus which are selected by the F2 function key. The F1 function key is the 'Help' key and the Escape key is used to quit any operation. Because the selection of every feature is from a menu there is no need for the familiar Control-C, Control-B two-key commands. F2 selects the menu and this is scrolled through by the up-arrow and down-arrow keys on the keypad.

The opening menu

The first menu to appear when WordStar 1512 is run, the command from the DOS prompt being

WS1512

It contains the options

```
Opening Menu

Word processing
Printing
Mailing list
List printing
Change settings
File management
Quit
Help
```

The highlight bar is moved through the options by means of the up and down arrow keys and the selection made by pressing Enter. Alternatively you can select your choice by pressing the first letter of the selection; W for wordprocessing, P for printing and so on. The top right hand corner of the screen reminds you of the keys to press if while that menu is driving the program; F1 for help, F2 for the next menu if the menu is large enough to be split into two parts, and Escape to 'Get out' as WordStar 1512 puts it!

Wordprocessing option
Choose the wordprocessing option and the WordStar 1512 Main Menu is displayed:

```
┌─────────────────────────────────────┐
│ Main Menu                           │
├─────────────────────────────────────┤
│ Edit current file                   │
│ Choose/create a file                │
│ Help index                          │
│                                     │
└─────────────────────────────────────┘
```

Edit current file accesses the last document worked on.

Choose/create a file allows you to choose a file to edit from the directory listing displayed, or create a fresh file with a name specified by you. You can choose a file from the directory listing by highlighting the name of the file. Up and down arrows are displayed at the top right hand corner of the screen to remind you that you can scroll through the list of available files in order to highlight the one required. WordStar 1512 allows the use of paths in a filename so that a filename such as

    B:\WP\JDLETTER\JLLETT1.DOC

is acceptable.

When a file is chosen to be edited, information is displayed on the screen telling you the drive and the directory it resides in, the date of the last update of that file, its size, the amount of space left on the disk and the printer currently in use. (This is called the *page layout* and WordStar 1512 allows you to configure the program to use up to three printers.)

Help index provides you with a list of the subjects available through help screens.

Once you have chosen a file to edit the 'typing screen' is displayed; shown in Figure 8. This consists of the typing area, a status line and a ruler line.

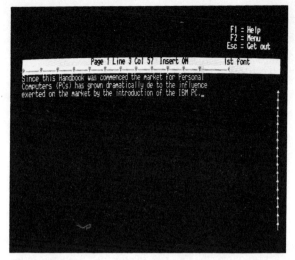

Figure 8

The status line displays the current page, line and column numbers together with information regarding the status of the document; INSERT OFF, for example.

The ruler line shows the position of the left and right margins and any tab settings.

The text is entered as with any other wordprocessor with the words wrapping round once the right hand margin has been reached.

Cursor movement is controlled in the following way:

← and → move the cursor left and right by one character.

Control with ← or → moves the cursor by one word left or right.

Control and **Home** moves the cursor to the beginning of the current line.

Control and **End** moves the cursor to the end of the current line.

Home moves the cursor to the top of the current screen.

End moves the cursor to the bottom of the current screen.

PgUp moves the display up by one 'screenful'.

PgDn moves the display down by one 'screenful'.

Control and **PgUp** moves you to the beginning of the document.

Control and **PgDn** moves you to the end of the document.

The **backspace** key deletes the character before the cursor and the **Del** key deletes the character under the cursor.

Shift and **backspace** deletes an entire line of text.

There are two editing menus available from the typing screen. The first is displayed by pressing the F2 function key and the second is displayed by pressing the key a second time.

```
┌─────────────────────────────────────┐
│ Editing Menu – 1 of 2               │
├─────────────────────────────────────┤
│ Boldface                            │
│ Underline                           │
│ Move text                           │
│ Copy text                           │
│ Delete text                         │
│ Restore deleted text                │
│ Temporary indent                    │
│ Paragraph re-form                   │
│ End page                            │
│ Save                                │
└─────────────────────────────────────┘
```

```
┌─────────────────────────────────────┐
│ Editing Menu – 2 of 2               │
├─────────────────────────────────────┤
│ Centre line                         │
│ Tabs and margins                    │
│ Find and replace                    │
│ Insert a file                       │
│ – Subscript                         │
│ + Superscript                       │
│ Pitch styles                        │
│ Line spacing                        │
│ Variable names                      │
│ Spelling correction                 │
└─────────────────────────────────────┘
```

The use of many of the options is self evident. All you need to do is to select the option you require, by moving the highlight or pressing B for Boldface, U for underline, etc, and follow the instructions displayed on the screen. Underlining, for example, is performed by moving the cursor to the start of the text to be underlined, pressing Enter, and then moving the cursor to the end of the text to be underlined and pressing Enter again.

When using **Find and replace** you are given the options +/− after entering the word to be found. A + sign indicates that you want to find the word and then replace it. If you enter − you only want to find the word. A further selection after the replacement word has been entered is another +/− option. The + is for automatic replacement without asking throughout the text. The − is for a query at every find with optional replacement. A new menu asks you if you want to Replace or Skip.

The typing screen is left by pressing Escape − always look at the top right hand corner of the screen for immediate help, press F1 for detailed help. Before you leave the typing screen you will be asked if you want to save the edited file (Save changes) or leave the file alone (Abandon changes). Select the one you require and you will be returned to the Main Menu.

The Variable names option is used in conjunction with the Maillist feature. WordStar 1512 provides you with a ready made data screen with a number of pre-defined fields. In order to insert these into a form letter to be merged with a data file you select this option and then chose your data field to be inserted in your letter. The Variable names screen is shown below:

```
Variable Names Menu

a  Record#        n  County
b  Date           o  Postcode
c  Mr/Ms          p  Country
d  Fullname       q  Phone-1
e  First          r  Phone-2
f  MI             s  Keyword-1
g  Last           t  Keyword-2
h  Last           u  Keyword-3
i  Title          v  Note-1
j  Company        w  Note-2
k  Address-1      x  Note-3
l  Address-2      y  Flag
m  Town
```

To create a form letter select the Choose/create a file option and display the typing screen. Press F2 twice to select the second editing menu and press V to select the Variable names sub-menu. Press b to select the date and move the cursor to the place where you want the date to be displayed in the letter. Then press the Enter key and you will see that

&date/o&

is displayed on the screen at that point. You can select any one of the 25 fields to be displayed in your letter in that way. Notice that the **Fullname** option, option **d** is made up of several fields from the data screen and saves you the trouble of having to combine them to create the full name of a person.

If you choose the Spelling correction option you will see that once the dictionary has been attached the spelling checker will commence to read through the file. As a suspected word is reached it will offer you a choice of alternatives. Your selection is made through the next menu:

```
┌─────────────────────────────────────┐
│ Spelling Correction                 │
├─────────────────────────────────────┤
│ Correct as suggested                │
│ Replace in entire file              │
│ Next suggestion                     │
│ Previous suggestion                 │
│ _ _ _ _ _ _ _ _ _ _ _ _ _           │
│ Type your correction                │
│ Add to your dictionary              │
│ Bypass this line                    │
│ Ignore in entire file               │
└─────────────────────────────────────┘
```

If you have chosen to type your own correction in
then a further menu is displayed:

```
┌─────────────────────────────────────┐
│ Spelling Correction                 │
├─────────────────────────────────────┤
│ Correct as typed                    │
│ Replace in entire file              │
│ Type a new correction               │
│ Bypass this time                    │
└─────────────────────────────────────┘
```

Printing option

```
┌─────────────────────────────────────┐
│ Print Menu                          │
├─────────────────────────────────────┤
│ Begin printing current file         │
│ Choose a file to print              │
│ Modify print options                │
│ Use another printer                 │
└─────────────────────────────────────┘
```

The first two choices on this menu are self explanatory. The Modify print options choice allows you to define such things as the number of the starting page and last page to be printed. The margin offset can be specified here as can the automatic numbering of pages.

The final option from this screen allows you to select one of three printers for use. WordStar 1512 provides you with the facility of describing three possible printers for use with your PC. It is at this point that you can choose which is to be used for printing the document.

Mailing list option

```
Maillist Main Menu

Begin data entry
Choose/create master list
Sort master list
Manage master lists
Help index
```

The data file used in conjunction with form letters is created from this menu. If you choose the second option you can create the data file, called a 'master list' by WordStar 1512, and the screen displayed is shown in Figure 9. After selecting the master list you go back to the menu and press **B** to begin the data entry. It is as simple as filling in a form with with a pen and paper. The data entry menu is shown below Figure 9.

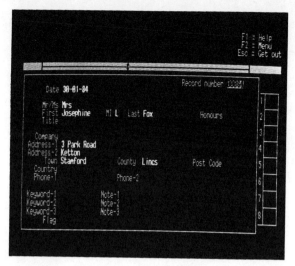

Figure 9

```
Data Entry Menu

Add record
Delete record
Begin search
End search
Customise data entry
Flag records
Update sublists
```

The master list can be searched by choosing the Begin search option. When you choose this a blank screen is displayed so that you can enter the criteria for the search on it. Control and Enter starts the search and once one matching record has been found **PgDn** will take you to the next record to match and so on through the file until the last matching record has been found. Then you must choose 'End search'.

You can save a certain amount of time in data entry by choosing the next option, Customise data entry. This allows you to put common data into every record, skip over certain fields that are not required or hide a field so that data cannot be entered into it.

A master list can be divided into a number of sublists based upon criteria chosen by you and these are chosen from this option. The instructions are displayed on the screen to help you.

A master list can be sorted on one of a number of fields and the choices are displayed in the Sort Menu shown next.

```
┌─────────────────────────┐
│  Sort Menu              │
├─────────────────────────┤
│  Record number          │
│  Date                   │
│  Name                   │
│  Company                │
│  County/town            │
│  Postcode               │
│  Phone-1                │
│  1st keyword            │
│  2nd keyword            │
│  3rd keyword            │
│  Flag                   │
└─────────────────────────┘
```

If you choose the **Manage Master Lists** option you are
presented with the following menu. The first two
options are designed to be used if your PC1512 has a
hard disk fitted.

When one or more records are deleted from a
master file they are actually only marked ready for
deletion. Purging the file from this menu performs the
final deletion of the records which up to that point have
only been marked as ready for deletion.

```
Manage Master Lists Menu

Backup a master list
Restore a master list
Purge deleted records
Name/rename sublists
Convert to ASCII format
Select master list
```

List printing option
This choice produces the following menu:

```
Maillist Print Menu

Begin printing
Choose records to print
Pick print format
Sort order for printing
Test paper alignment
Modify print options
Use another printer
```

Begin printing starts printing the selected items.
Choose records to print provides you with a screen
from which you can choose to print an entire master
file, flagged records only or one of the sublists of the
master file.

Pick print format allows you to choose the style of printing from the following menu

```
┌─────────────────────────────┐
│ Print Format Menu           │
├─────────────────────────────┤
│ Letters                     │
│ Mailing labels              │
│ Envelopes                   │
│ Telephone directory         │
│ Proof report                │
│ Rotary cards                │
└─────────────────────────────┘
```

Letters allows you to merge print the master file, flagged records or sublists with a letter created using the wordprocessor.

Mailing labels provides you with a further menu of choices to select the printing of mailing labels in one-across, two-across or four-across formats.

Mailing Labels Menu		
Small	one-across	($3\frac{1}{2} \times 1$)
Medium	one-across	($4 \times 1\frac{1}{2}$)
Large	one-across	(5×3)
Cheshire	four-across	($3\frac{1}{2} \times 1$)
$3\frac{1}{2} \times 1$	two-across	
$4 \times 1\frac{1}{2}$	two-across	

Envelopes will allow you to print names and addresses on envelopes which can be either hand fed into your printer or continuous form envelopes.

Telephone directory will print out a list of the names in your master list, or selections from it, together with the relevant telephone numbers.

Proof report prints the contents of every field of each record in a master file, or selections from it.

Rotary cards will produce names, addresses and telephone numbers on continuous feed filing cards.

Sort order for printing provides you with the same sort menu as was provided when you sorted a master file.

Test paper alignment prints dummy data in the form of a series of xs on your labels in order to allow you to check that the labels have been loaded into the printer in the correct place. You can then adjust the position of the paper before proceeding with the printing proper.

Modify print options offers you the same choices of pages to be printed as, for example, for the printing of a conventional wordprocessed document.

Use another printer allows you to select one of the other two printers WordStar 1512 allows you to configure as part of the system.

Change settings option
The Change Settings Menu is shown below:

```
Change Settings Menu

Wordprocessing settings
Mailing list settings
Drive/directory
Page layout
Set up printers
Customise printers
```

Wordprocessing settings produces the following menu:

```
Word Processing Settings

Insert mode
Justification
Prompts
Document mode
Auto-reform
Find/replace whole words only
Find/replace case sensitive
```

The choices are made by moving to the appropriate line with the arrow keys and pressing the + key. A tick will appear to the left of the selection to show that this has been done. To delete the tick, and hence the selection, move the highlight to the selection to be deleted and press the Del key.

Mailing list settings produces the following menu:

```
Mailing List Settings

Display sublist boxes
Show sublist names
Case sensitive search
Beeps during data entry
```

Again, these selections are made by pressing the + key or the Del key to accept or reject a setting.

Drive/directory allows you to specify the drive and directory where your main files are located.

Page layout allows you to define the layout of the pages to be printed by each of the three printers selectable by the system. It gives you freedom to choose the left and right hand margin sizes, the top and bottom margins and the position of the page numbers.

Set up printers is used when you want to select the printers to be used on your system. Over 200 printers are available for selection from the WordStar 1512 options.

Customise printers gives you the ability to select special features, such as fonts of characters and character spacing, for each one of your three selected printers.

File management option

```
┌─────────────────────────────┐
│ File Management Menu        │
│                             │
│ Copy                        │
│ Move                        │
│ Rename                      │
│ Delete                      │
│                             │
└─────────────────────────────┘
```

This option covers certain 'housekeeping' functions carried out on your WordStar files.

Dot commands in text

As with the 'standard' WordStar there are a number of 'dot' commands that can be embedded in the text. For the editing and printing of text the following commands are available:

.FM (n) footer margin
.FO (text) one line footer
.HE (text) one line header text
.HM (n) header margin
.LH (n) line height (6 – 8 lpi, 8 – 6 lpi, 12 – 4 lpi, 16 – 3 lpi, 24 – 2 lpi)
.LM (n) left margin
.MB (n) bottom margin
.MT (n) top margin

.OJ (on/off/dis) on, off or at your discretion

.OP page no off

.PA page break

.PC(n) page column for page number

.PF (on/off/dis) paragraph format – on, off or at your discretion

.PL (n) page length

.PN (n) page number

.PO(n) page offset

.RM (n) right margin

.CP (n) conditional break – commands that the next **n** lines must be kept together on a page

.IG non-printing line – used for comments. Has the same effect as a line commencing with **..**

When the **Maillist** option has been chosen the following dot commands can be used.

.AV (variable) ask for a variable to be inserted in your document at print time

.CS clear screen

.DM (message) display message on the screen at print time

.IF (cond) conditional statement IF

.EX (condition) conditional statement – EXCEPT (These conditional statements can include .OR., .AND. logical expressions.)

.EF end condition

.FI file insert – inserts a file at this point at print time

.RP (n) repeat document **n** times – used with mail merging by selecting the first **n** records from the data file to be merge printed

.SV (var name, substitution) set variables to be included in your print document at print time

Index